HAL•LEONARD

EASY INSTRUMENTAL PLAY-ALONG

Audio Access Included

POP FAVORITES FOR TROMBONE

CONTENTS

To access audio visit:
www.halleonard.com/mylibrary

Enter Code
7957-4033-2116-1951

Audio Arrangements by Peter Deneff
Tracking, mixing, and mastering by BeatHouse Music

ISBN 978-1-4950-9269-5

HAL•LEONARD®

7777 W. BLUEMOUND RD. P.O. BOX 13819 MILWAUKEE, WI 53213

Visit Hal Leonard Online at
www.halleonard.com

ACHY BREAKY HEART
(Don't Tell My Heart)

Words and Music by
DON VON TRESS

I'M A BELIEVER

Words and Music by
NEIL DIAMOND

LA BAMBA

By RITCHIE VALENS

LOUIE, LOUIE

Words and Music by
RICHARD BERRY

Moderately

Electric piano

IMAGINE

Words and Music by
JOHN LENNON

JAILHOUSE ROCK

Words and Music by JERRY LEIBER
and MIKE STOLLER

OB-LA-DI, OB-LA-DA

Words and Music by JOHN LENNON
and PAUL McCARTNEY

SPLISH SPLASH

Words and Music by BOBBY DARIN
and MURRAY KAUFMAN

STAND BY ME

Words and Music by JERRY LEIBER,
MIKE STOLLER and BEN E. KING

YELLOW SUBMARINE

Words and Music by JOHN LENNON
and PAUL McCARTNEY

Shuffle feel

Audio Access Included

HAL•LEONARD
EASY INSTRUMENTAL PLAY-ALONG

- Perfect for beginning players
- Carefully edited to include only the notes and rhythms that students learn in the first months playing their instrument

- Great-sounding demonstration and play-along tracks
- Audio tracks can be accessed online for download or streaming, using the unique code inside the book

DISNEY
Book with Online Audio Tracks

The Ballad of Davy Crockett • Can You Feel the Love Tonight • Candle on the Water • I Just Can't Wait to Be King • The Medallion Calls • Mickey Mouse March • Part of Your World • Whistle While You Work • You Can Fly! You Can Fly! You Can Fly! • You'll Be in My Heart (Pop Version).

00122184	Flute	$9.99
00122185	Clarinet	$9.99
00122186	Alto Sax	$9.99
00122187	Tenor Sax	$9.99
00122188	Trumpet	$9.99
00122189	Horn	$9.99
00122190	Trombone	$9.99
00122191	Violin	$9.99
00122192	Viola	$9.99
00122193	Cello	$9.99
00122194	Keyboard Percussion	$9.99

CLASSIC ROCK
Book with Online Audio Tracks

Another One Bites the Dust • Born to Be Wild • Brown Eyed Girl • Dust in the Wind • Every Breath You Take • Fly like an Eagle • I Heard It Through the Grapevine • I Shot the Sheriff • Oye Como Va • Up Around the Bend.

00122195	Flute	$9.99
00122196	Clarinet	$9.99
00122197	Alto Sax	$9.99
00122198	Tenor Sax	$9.99
00122201	Trumpet	$9.99
00122202	Horn	$9.99
00122203	Trombone	$9.99
00122205	Violin	$9.99
00122206	Viola	$9.99
00122207	Cello	$9.99
00122208	Keyboard Percussion	$9.99

CLASSICAL THEMES
Book with Online Audio Tracks

Can Can • Carnival of Venice • Finlandia • Largo from Symphony No. 9 ("New World") • Morning • Musette in D Major • Ode to Joy • Spring • Symphony No. 1 in C Minor, Fourth Movement Excerpt • Trumpet Voluntary.

00123108	Flute	$9.99
00123109	Clarinet	$9.99
00123110	Alto Sax	$9.99
00123111	Tenor Sax	$9.99
00123112	Trumpet	$9.99
00123113	Horn	$9.99
00123114	Trombone	$9.99
00123115	Violin	$9.99
00123116	Viola	$9.99
00123117	Cello	$9.99
00123118	Keyboard Percussion	$9.99

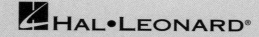

HAL•LEONARD®

www.halleonard.com

HAL•LEONARD INSTRUMENTAL PLAY-ALONG

Your favorite songs are arranged just for solo instrumentalists with this outstanding series. Each book includes a great full-accompaniment play-along audio so you can sound just like a pro! Check out **www.halleonard.com** to see all the titles available.

The Beatles

All You Need Is Love • Blackbird • Day Tripper • Eleanor Rigby • Get Back • Here, There and Everywhere • Hey Jude • I Will • Let It Be • Lucy in the Sky with Diamonds • Ob-La-Di, Ob-La-Da • Penny Lane • Something • Ticket to Ride • Yesterday.

___ 00225330	Flute	$14.99
___ 00225331	Clarinet	$14.99
___ 00225332	Alto Sax	$14.99
___ 00225333	Tenor Sax	$14.99
___ 00225334	Trumpet	$14.99
___ 00225335	Horn	$14.99
___ 00225336	Trombone	$14.99
___ 00225337	Violin	$14.99
___ 00225338	Viola	$14.99
___ 00225339	Cello	$14.99

Chart Hits

All About That Bass • All of Me • Happy • Radioactive • Roar • Say Something • Shake It Off • A Sky Full of Stars • Someone like You • Stay with Me • Thinking Out Loud • Uptown Funk.

___ 00146207	Flute	$12.99
___ 00146208	Clarinet	$12.99
___ 00146209	Alto Sax	$12.99
___ 00146210	Tenor Sax	$12.99
___ 00146211	Trumpet	$12.99
___ 00146212	Horn	$12.99
___ 00146213	Trombone	$12.99
___ 00146214	Violin	$12.99
___ 00146215	Viola	$12.99
___ 00146216	Cello	$12.99

Coldplay

Clocks • Every Teardrop Is a Waterfall • Fix You • In My Place • Lost! • Paradise • The Scientist • Speed of Sound • Trouble • Violet Hill • Viva La Vida • Yellow.

___ 00103337	Flute	$12.99
___ 00103338	Clarinet	$12.99
___ 00103339	Alto Sax	$12.99
___ 00103340	Tenor Sax	$12.99
___ 00103341	Trumpet	$12.99
___ 00103342	Horn	$12.99
___ 00103343	Trombone	$12.99
___ 00103344	Violin	$12.99
___ 00103345	Viola	$12.99
___ 00103346	Cello	$12.99

Disney Greats

Arabian Nights • Hawaiian Roller Coaster Ride • It's a Small World • Look Through My Eyes • Yo Ho (A Pirate's Life for Me) • and more.

___ 00841934	Flute	$12.99
___ 00841935	Clarinet	$12.99
___ 00841936	Alto Sax	$12.99
___ 00841937	Tenor Sax	$12.95
___ 00841938	Trumpet	$12.99
___ 00841939	Horn	$12.99
___ 00841940	Trombone	$12.95
___ 00841941	Violin	$12.99
___ 00841942	Viola	$12.99
___ 00841943	Cello	$12.99
___ 00842078	Oboe	$12.99

Great Themes

Bella's Lullaby • Chariots of Fire • Get Smart • Hawaii Five-O Theme • I Love Lucy • The Odd Couple • Spanish Flea • and more.

___ 00842468	Flute	$12.99
___ 00842469	Clarinet	$12.99
___ 00842470	Alto Sax	$12.99
___ 00842471	Tenor Sax	$12.99
___ 00842472	Trumpet	$12.99
___ 00842473	Horn	$12.99
___ 00842474	Trombone	$12.99
___ 00842475	Violin	$12.99
___ 00842476	Viola	$12.99
___ 00842477	Cello	$12.99

Popular Hits

Breakeven • Fireflies • Halo • Hey, Soul Sister • I Gotta Feeling • I'm Yours • Need You Now • Poker Face • Viva La Vida • You Belong with Me • and more.

___ 00842511	Flute	$12.99
___ 00842512	Clarinet	$12.99
___ 00842513	Alto Sax	$12.99
___ 00842514	Tenor Sax	$12.99
___ 00842515	Trumpet	$12.99
___ 00842516	Horn	$12.99
___ 00842517	Trombone	$12.99
___ 00842518	Violin	$12.99
___ 00842519	Viola	$12.99
___ 00842520	Cello	$12.99

Songs from Frozen, Tangled and Enchanted

Do You Want to Build a Snowman? • For the First Time in Forever • Happy Working Song • I See the Light • In Summer • Let It Go • Mother Knows Best • That's How You Know • True Love's First Kiss • When Will My Life Begin • and more.

___ 00126921	Flute	$14.99
___ 00126922	Clarinet	$14.99
___ 00126923	Alto Sax	$14.99
___ 00126924	Tenor Sax	$14.99
___ 00126925	Trumpet	$14.99
___ 00126926	Horn	$14.99
___ 00126927	Trombone	$14.99
___ 00126928	Violin	$14.99
___ 00126929	Viola	$14.99
___ 00126930	Cello	$14.99

Top Hits

Adventure of a Lifetime • Budapest • Die a Happy Man • Ex's & Oh's • Fight Song • Hello • Let It Go • Love Yourself • One Call Away • Pillowtalk • Stitches • Writing's on the Wall.

___ 00171073	Flute	$12.99
___ 00171074	Clarinet	$12.99
___ 00171075	Alto Sax	$12.99
___ 00171106	Tenor Sax	$12.99
___ 00171107	Trumpet	$12.99
___ 00171108	Horn	$12.99
___ 00171109	Trombone	$12.99
___ 00171110	Violin	$12.99
___ 00171111	Viola	$12.99
___ 00171112	Cello	$12.99

Wicked

As Long As You're Mine • Dancing Through Life • Defying Gravity • For Good • I'm Not That Girl • Popular • The Wizard and I • and more.

___ 00842236	Flute	$12.99
___ 00842237	Clarinet	$12.99
___ 00842238	Alto Saxophone	$11.95
___ 00842239	Tenor Saxophone	$11.95
___ 00842240	Trumpet	$11.99
___ 00842241	Horn	$11.95
___ 00842242	Trombone	$12.99
___ 00842243	Violin	$11.99
___ 00842244	Viola	$12.99
___ 00842245	Cello	$12.99

HAL•LEONARD®

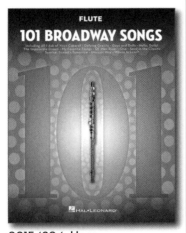
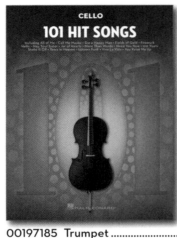

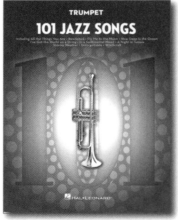